A Late Return

William Rees makes a precarious living by selling used books. He has worked as a reporter for a local newspaper in London and ran a bookshop in Bangor before the lure of travel, bookselling and a woman in France led him to take a less conventional path. His memoir, *The Loneliness of the Long Distance Book Runner*, was a runaway hit.

In recent years, Bill has rediscovered the joys and frustrations of competitive table tennis. An embarrassingly large amount of his time and energies have been devoted to perfecting his backhand top spin. *A Late Return* goes some way to explaining why.

A Late Return

Table tennis à la carte

William Rees

Parthian, Cardigan SA43 1ED
www.parthianbooks.com
First published in Great Britain by Parthian
© Bill Rees 2021
All Rights Reserved
ISBN 978-1-913640-30-9
eISBN 978-1-913640-41-5
Cover design and typesetting by Syncopated Pandemonium
Cover and interior illustrations by Beach
Printed and bound by 4Edge in the UK
Published with the financial support of the Welsh Books
Council.
British Library Cataloguing in Publication Data
A cataloguing record for this book is available from the British
Library.

For my Le Vigan teammates

Ping-pong is a life style, a training in attention, a diversion, a mad passion and a way of not taking anything important too seriously and taking some tiny things much too seriously.

Pico Iyer

Tourists and locals are watching from sidewalk cafés. Non-racers. The emptiness of those lives shocks me.

The Rider by Tim Krabbé

Attack early, not rashly.

Simon of Le Vigan

Alain is not one to prolong a rally. Like a good boxer he hits hard with high precision. Many shots land as outright winners. And shots that opponents do return seldom cause him problems. He simply hits hard once more. Go fetch! That the ball will be returned again is most improbable.

Adjusting to Alain's pace of play is difficult. His speed of shot unsettles. Hurried into errors, opponents start doubting themselves. They start missing *sitters*. Ignominy ensues and defeat looms. I know because I've been there, on the – quite literally – receiving end.

Sport is about making better use of time than your adversary. On many levels Alain knows this. He is a fast closer of games. Before opponents know it, a chunky, sandy-haired figure is perfunctorily shaking their hand. Thirty-three points, rapidly amassed over three sets, to Monsieur Alain Fabre. So reads the scorecard, but really he should have one of those hooligan calling cards to give out: Congratulations! You have met Alain Fabre and joined the ranks of his time-starved victims.

Usually it is a quick death. Defeat, I mean.

*

Whether playing table tennis or having a conversation, Alain likes to get to the point quickly. Making or winning it.

For Alain, finishing things fast is a life credo. Driving included. Behind the wheel of his ancient red Peugeot estate, Alain is more of a Senna than a Prost, propelling it at engine protesting revs. On match Sundays it feels as though I get to partake in an additional sport, that of rally driving. Often I am in the front seat; an honorary co-pilot who – in lieu of classic navigational duties – is on the lookout for speed cameras and gendarmes.

This morning we speed – incurring no fines – to Mèze, a small Mediterranean town on the edge of the Étang de Thau, arriving with oodles of *guess what* to spare. Yes, Alain always makes sure it is on his side. Time, time, time, time's on his side, yes it is, as the Rolling Stones have raucously declaimed.

Our destination is a school gym. We find it easily. As have many other men like us desperate to recall the sporting thrills of their lithe youth.

Some remain inside parked cars, possibly engaged in last-minute meditation exercises. So as to be mentally fit for a sport once memorably described as chess on steroids. Not that I am making any special claims regarding the IQs of its practitioners. Least of all mine.

Obviously ping-pong is not as cerebral as chess. There are, though, certain similarities, like the kind of pain they both generate. That of losing versus that of thinking. You suffer one or the other or even both. It can be sheer mental turmoil. This is the downside of the deal. There is an upside, though. Mental ecstasy. Otherwise nobody would play.

As with chess some people question whether table tennis is a proper sport. To them I say: you cannot simultaneously play table tennis and puff on a fag. It is a SPORT, even if you do not have to be exceptionally sporty to play it.

*

In searching for a parking space, Alain drives with un-characteristic circumspection. To avoid mowing down the competition. Definitely against the rules, that.

— *Fais gaffe*! I shout, forcing Alain to brake. Crossing our path is a hulk of a man. He would take some knocking down even by a car. The hulk, I now notice, is fulsomely bearded and waving demonically at us. Alain waves back.

— It's Galtier. Said he couldn't play, the lying bastard.

Alain winds down his window, cutting the ignition.

— Miracle cure?

— No, the knee's still playing up, but someone's got to stop you. You winning would be a travesty.

Their banter belies their determination to triumph today. Indeed, in order to do so, both men will strain every muscle, sinew and neurone.

The joshing between them ceases, principally because of some poor sod stuck in a sky-blue Twingo. With his paunch caught on the steering wheel, he is making quite a (comic book) spectacle of himself. For a few seconds, utter confusion reigns, owing to a burst of frenzied hooting. Its source we first think must be the floundering fatty. But the noise is actually being generated by an angry man whose Sprinter van is unable to move, let alone sprint. Alain has inadvertently blocked it in.

Raising an arm in apology, Alain revs up his Peugeot, making Galtier jump clear of both us and the Sprinter van. He does so with surprising agility. Surprising, that is, for a giant with a dodgy knee. I say as much.

— Bad knee my arse, says Alain.

David chuckles in the back. As do I until I see a parking space.

— Here. Here.

I get overly excited about Alain filling it with his unlikely racing machine. Must be nerves.

From the boot Alain and I retrieve our bags, leaving David slouched on the back seats. David intends to sleep away most of the time between now and the start of the tournament. This represents quite a challenge when your pillow is a lumpy kit bag. Just as well David is able to nod off almost at will. He is a sleeping maestro. Does he dream of bamboozling opponents with fiendish serves of reverse, side and top spin?

I do. Overgrown schoolboy that I am.

On most Sundays, for the league matches, we are a four-man team. Marco the kid, a 29-year-old plumber, sitting alongside David in the car. Marco is a left hander, an all-out attacker in the Alain mould. Only he is not as good.

Marco plays like a machine with one setting. Flat out. Minimal finesse.

Ça passe ou ça casse. It is a machine that regularly breaks down, and tends to function – with a high degree of accuracy – only against opponents with fast serves. His style is fast and furious. There is no fury in Alain's game. Fury implies a certain imprecision and hot headedness. Alain is none of those things, especially when he has a table-tennis ball to strike and an opponent to outfox.

A louche bunch of blokes, piled into an accident scarred Peugeot, driven fast into the suburbs of Nîmes early morning, and leaving several hours later.

What must locals watching from rundown cafés think of them?

What illegalities must they be getting up to?

One, who asked for directions, even has a funny accent.

Table tennis, m' Lud. We were playing table tennis.

Sporting pursuits, you say.

True, we would swear. And here is why. Because it feels so good, the delicious simplicity of shrinking a Sunday morning to bat, table and ball.

*

Off amble Alain and I towards the sports hall's principal entrance where there is an unofficial assembly of tracksuit-clad men who are mostly in their forties and fifties. Acquaintances are being renewed, old rivalries rekindled. Nobody's hand goes unshaken. Everybody

addressed informally (using the tu form) belonging as
we all do to the brotherhood of pongistes.

— Salut.

— Salut.

I greet with one hand, using the other to shield my
eyes from the sun's glare. My skin prickles in the preco-
cious morning heat. Mèze, despite its southerly latitude,
shouldn't be this hot at this hour in May.

— Here we go, says Alain, rather portentously.

Upon entering the building we immediately detect a
sharp drop in temperature. The air-conditioned hall, a
merciful refuge from the climate outside. I am prepared
to overlook the ecological irony here, all my thoughts
focused on the rows and rows of navy-blue tables, and
the grown-ups in shorts wielding bats in their vicinity.
Engaged in mundane warm-up drills, about each and
every player there is an air of unmistakable accomplish-
ment. I suffer from an attack of imposter syndrome,
my body flushing with sudden nauseous panic. I make
myself look elsewhere and, in so doing, take in all the
orange plastic chairs which delineate non-playing areas.
Kit bags and bottles of water abound. I become acutely
aware of noise – generated by repeatedly struck balls –
there in the background. It is unremitting. Balls plock.
On tables, off bats. Plock. Plock. Plock . . .

I assume the author Howard Jacobson invented plock, an onomatopoeia nicely capturing the plasticky bounce of a ball on table or bat. Plock appears in his semi-autobiographical novel, *The Mighty Walzer*, about Jewish boys growing up in Manchester during the 1950s. The main character has a penchant and no little talent for playing table tennis. I loved that table tennis featured so prominently in this book. A renewed obsession with the sport having led me to seek out any literature associated with it. There is little to be found. There is, however, a rare book I'd like to get my hands on, which is a strange and intriguing collaboration; that of the writers and ping-pong enthusiasts, Pico Iyer and Geoff Dyer, responding to the 'vernacular ping-pong photographs' of Alec Soth. Unfortunately it has scarcity and cult value, and to acquire a copy you must cough up, at the very least, a quarter of a grand sterling.

*

Alain approvingly surveys the hall. The windows are high, through which light diffuses unobtrusively. There is an absence of distracting reflections, the tables glare free. Perfect playing conditions.

— Wasted on the kids, says Alain.

Only half joking, I suspect.

*

At a nearby table a grizzled septuagenarian, a V4, whose temple pulses visibly, is hitting the ball with such venom as to make me wonder why I had bothered to come and play. His shots would make mincemeat of any defence I could offer. Alain reads my thoughts.

— He's pre-match flash happy. Bet you he won't be playing like that in the matches.

I hope Alain is right, that playing with the *élan* of the carefree is nigh impossible in a competitive encounter.

V4s are rare and hardy birds indeed. Alain, David and I are V2s. The majority of entrants are V1s.

Alain knows most of the players whose multifarious strengths and weaknesses he précises for my benefit.

— Specko's master of angles with a deceptively tricky serve. But he loses his rag easily and then disintegrates . . .

— Alain, I've got glasses.

— Yeah, well . . . There's Misha. Uses a non-sponge bat, old style. You've got to be patient. Let him make the mistakes. Has a tendency to make sluggish returns. Milo's got a brilliant forehand, but mediocre backhand you must target. Gérard's lacklustre demeanour is a guise. There's fire in his belly, you just can't see it till it's too late. Loves winning more than me! There's Balkoney, the skinny bloke with a wispy beard, big smoker, cranky, defends well and is a total wanker. There's Fat Bernie, clad ambitiously in a tracksuit, got a mad temper on him, so easily provoked.

We see that the man stuck in the Twingo has extricated himself. He is fatter even than Fat Bernie, but boy does he strike a clean ball. Alain and I exchange looks of amazement. In warming up he is displaying a disconcerting speed of shot and regularity. Making him a contender, I think. Alain thinks not.

— No puff.

We gravitate towards the refreshment stall, cloaking ourselves in the aroma of croissants and fresh coffee. Pinned to the wall behind is the draw, an innocuous-looking piece of paper. Yet it holds our respective destinies for this morning, and is thus worthy of a thorough inspection. Alain puts ticks against our names, this being standard protocol to register a player's presence. Others have done likewise. Alain wonders aloud if he should put a semi-tick for David.

— Assuming he's going to wake up in time!

Alain smirks. He points to David's pool.

— Look who he's got first game.

I look. He has got Galtier.

— David can knock him out for me.

Yeah, yeah, Alain. Very funny.

Alain points to another player in David's pool.

— Miguel Sanchez. Hairy arms. Good player, says Alain.

For Alain to say so makes him a very good player.

We turn to my pool. I don't recognise any players, which is hardly a surprise. This being my first regional. What I can't fail to see, however, is that the players I am to face have points ratings considerably higher than mine (920). This indicates their superiority. Alain tries to reassure me that a disparity in our respective rankings counts for little in a competition like today's.

— And you can turn them to your advantage. Remember they have more to lose than you.

True, I think. The winner is who technically gets first to eleven points. This is not always or necessarily the better player. This 'underdog may triumph' theory, though, has a sting in its tail. It allows for the possibility of inferior ranked players defeating me! Stop it, Bill. Banish the defeatist thoughts.

What was it that Woody Allen said about success? It being mostly about showing up. Cleverly comic, yes, but do these words of comfort contain one ounce of truth?

*

Alain notes the players in his pool. He does not seem unduly perturbed even though Shyler is the only name he recognises.

— Used to be good, now he's past it.

We go off to locate a free table. Some guys, realising we are waiting to practise, graciously cede their table to us.

From my bag I remove a bat whose sponge is shiny new. I brought my fast new weapon, a Balsa Tibhar blade with bespoke Andro Shifter sponges, to training sessions this last week and its extra speed wreaked havoc against everyone save Alain. Simon, our club coach, was very approving.

— Fuel injection, Bill. Like the fuel injection.

Despite having no driving licence, Simon has a predilection for motoring metaphors.

My mind has recourse to two instruments, a body and a bat. I have no choice but to play with the body that my parents created. The bat, though, is something I can select. Yet this autonomy brings with it doubt over whether a new bat might let me down? Ultra-fineness of touch requires a level of intimacy I enjoy only with my old bat. So what is it to be? Earlier I had aired my dilemma on the way to Mèze. We had been zooming along a virtually vacant stretch of motorway.

— Out with the old, in with the new.

This was Alain's view and I had not dissented. But the new bat, in my hand, feels like foreign tissue. I swop it for a bat whose rubber edges are worn and frayed, like the nerves of its owner. I rub a ball on the rubber, convincing myself that it still has sufficient grip. Oldie it is to be. The handle long since worn smooth by my grip.

In my head I hear Simon exhorting Alain and me to 'get our diesels going'. Rightly so. The playing conditions seem great, but we still need to become accustomed to them. The quality of light, the acoustics, the feel of the floor beneath our trainers.

Forehand to forehand, backhand to backhand, slowly to begin with, allowing ourselves the time to acquire rhythm. My mood buoys, the ball passing over the net with increasing accuracy and speed. It is as though I have entered into a trance. My body hits the ball and I do nothing to stop it!

Nervous tension diffuses with the retrieval of muscle memory. I anticipate his shots, he anticipates mine. Our movements a harmonized whole until Alain fires a shot towards the table centre and I fail to make the necessary adjustment.

Next we do the butterfly, meaning I do the lines, Alain the diagonals; the ball thereby tracing the imagined wings of a perversely angular and gigantic butterfly. We swop with me doing diagonals, Alain the lines. I make fewer mistakes hitting diagonal shots. There's more table to play with, greater margin for error. Basic geometry, really. Shapes and angles being the foundational essence of a sport comprising a plastic white sphere and a rectangular table and net. Nice and basic like the windows of Play School.

I, too, must adjust the shape of my body and bat to the rhythm of my opponent. So Simon advises. Between matches the player must 'retune the engine'. The engine being a two stroke: relax (between shots), explode (while executing a shot). Relax, explode. Relax, explode.

Warming up I am focusing hard on my shots, oblivious to the sounds of rallies coming from neighbouring tables. I am about to play my first regional *criterium*. Get to the final and you qualify for the nationals! This is a big deal. *Occitanie's* best *vétérans* are here. All primed to do battle with bat and ball.

*

8.20 a.m.

David shows up.

— Wasn't a beauty sleep then, says Alain.

— Ha ha.

Alain heads off for a coffee. I remain at the table with David who is suddenly desperately keen to practise. This season his win rate is fractionally below 50 per cent. From the way he plays, you'd expect it to be higher. David is a slight man, and classically correct in his choice of shot. That he regularly loses to players with ugly styles is difficult to fathom. Alain attributes such defeats to David's laidbackness.

David is my doubles partner. We play well together,

especially against those youngsters who tend to overly attack. Alain usually plays with Marco because he is good enough to make up for his partner's shortcomings. I dislike playing with Alain. Lumbered with a less talented partner, he does not bother to conceal his frustration. One of his and Simon's pet hates is meekly returning the ball when it is there to be smashed off the table. It is a golden rule of theirs: Thou shall not play diffidently.

— Bill. How many times must I have to tell you? I'd rather you missed a smash then you just keep the ball in play. Any decent opponents will punish you straightaway.

*

8.30 a.m. Organisers' call

We are officially welcomed by the tournament referee, a stern-faced lady who is sitting rigidly at a table laden with laptops and disparate sheets of paper. She apologises for having a cold and then briskly runs through the rules. Shorts are deemed an absolute must. Foul language will result in instant disqualification. No coaching from the side-lines. Matches are to be umpired by players in the same pool. And no – absolutely no – eating in the playing areas.

Am I the only person listening attentively to the croakily voiced dos and do nots? I have that impression. The others have probably heard it all before.

8.40 a.m. Five minutes before tournament start.

David is eating dried banana.

— Want some?

— No thanks.

Bananas give me indigestion. This may be psychosomatic. Linked to an embarrassing incident that happened in a supermarket last year. Having just bought some groceries I was stopped from leaving by a shop detective, asking to look in my bag. It contained a single banana, which I had packed before training. I had quite forgotten it was there.

— Is this yours or ours.

— Mine.

— Sure?

— Yes.

This was ridiculous, but I felt it necessary to explain how the banana came to be in my bag. We were near to the fruit counter, and I could see a whole heap of green bananas.

— Look. Mine's yellow. Do you think it ripened between there and the check-out stall.

Despite feeling hot and very bothered, I was playing as if for laughs.

— Leave your bag at the entrance next time.

No wise cracks Bill, no wise cracks. Say nothing and leave.

I did as I told myself. Phew.

I believe in the power of porridge! That a substantial bowl of it should suffice until lunch. Although – for emergency supplies of energy – I have figs and chocolate in my bag. Between sets I do not snack much. I do, however, always have a water bottle to hand. I swig regularly so as to stay hydrated. Simon compares body hydration to oil level in a car engine. Dehydration is a pet hate of his.

— No excuse for the body breaking down. No excuse.

Alain likes to breakfast on jam-spread bread and croissants. He probably wolfed down (another) croissant with his coffee just now. Lucky with his metabolism, he can almost eat anything and still play great table tennis.

Early morning is all about the pool stages. Players who finish top and second go through to the afternoon's knockout stage. So finishing second is not disastrous. Just make sure that you don't finish third or fourth, warned Alain. Thanks Alain. Expert advice, that. As if David and I are entirely responsible for our respective fates. It would be nice to have Alain's confidence. For that matter it would be nice to have his experience and ability. Yet for all Alain's undoubted superiority, there are times in training when his radar is not fully functioning, and I get exceptionally lucky. I thereby register sweet victories. These wins are rare and unexpected, but they are wins nonetheless, illustrative of the unpredictability of sporting contests. Importantly, they allow an exaggerated belief in my playing potential. I enter competitions thinking I can defeat Alain and players of his ilk. I am far from alone. At the day's start there is a huge collective reservoir of hope, one which inexorably diminishes as the competition proceeds and reality bites. Players thus confronted by the misalignment between personal credence and the actual probability of victory.

A salient fact. There can only be one winner. Here is another. Only the finalists qualify for the nationals.

What is a good collective noun for middle-aged men with high sporting ambitions?

A frustration. A delusion.

Take your pick.

I still remember the shock of going for a run with my son who had just turned fifteen. How had he become suddenly so fast? Why was I so slow, so very laboured in my running gait. I did not want to accept that I was ageing.

Table tennis is kinder to non-youthful limbs and minds. The ageing process less visible. The physical distances involved in playing the sport are shorter. You may nurture the inner Peter Pan.

I clean my bat and neurotically retie my laces. David puts on the club shirt which is white with large dark lettering of the club's sponsor, a local Citroën dealer (Simon's choice!). Alain says his shirt is in the wash. So is mine, I lie. I find its collar restrictive, preferring a looser fitting T-shirt, but not so loose as to snag on my bat, which can happen against opponents who target the body.

*

The tournament organisers do their best to ensure that players from the same club will not meet each other in the pool stages. So before proceeding to our assigned tables, Alain, David and I genuinely wish each other the best of luck. We leave our gear on three orange chairs aligned on the far side of the hall, a base camp of sorts, to where we will return after playing to offer and receive congratulations or commiserations, depending on our results.

Off I go to table four, on the front row of tables. Across from these tables there is space for players and coaches to congregate. There is even room for neutral spectators. Apparently an article appeared in yesterday's *Midi Libre*, inviting the general public to attend the tournament. I don't see anyone yet who is not directly involved in playing. Perhaps people will come for the knockout stages late morning.

Our coach is absent today. Simon is celebrating his son's birthday. This was actually last week. Alain is a little peeved by Simon's absence. I, though, am not unhappy. Simon's interventions at tournaments put me on edge. David probably doesn't mind, one way or the other.

*

They are waiting for me, all three adversaries in my pool. One, as bald as I am, must be in his fifties. A fellow V2 but with a 1300 rating. The other two are V1s (1100 and

1360). One in a Fred Perry top and Adidas shorts. The other wears a Marseille top bearing the name of Vernon.

V (as in V1, 2, 3 & 4) stands for veteran. I think of making a joke about the superiority of V2 missiles, the ones that Hitler had hoped would force Britain to surrender. I desist. The intended humour I fear is not easily translatable. I would use up too much energy in attempting a translation. Energy I can ill afford to squander. Table tennis can be a real drain on the mental as well as physical reserves.

*

I am to play the V2 first. We shake hands.

— Michel.

— Bill.

All he says is that he hails from Montpellier. Why exactly, I do not know. Am I meant to be impressed by this banal fact of geography?

I do not like the look of the bat Michel is brandishing like a revolver.

It has long pips! I lack practise against decent exponents of the long pip game.

Players who make the ball seriously misbehave.

Our club players who use long pips aren't particularly proficient. Bertrand defends reasonably well but does not attack. Baptiste is given to playing overambitious shots.

Earlier against Alain and David, I was hitting the ball cleanly. Now my timing is off. Michel from Montpellier uses a conventional inverted rubber for the backhand, which poses scant difficulty unlike the long pips on his forehand that reverse the spin on the ball. In the warm-up he sees this and wants to start the match as soon as possible.

— Ready?

— A little more.

I intend to use the full five minutes allotted for warming up.

They pass all too quickly.

— Good match, he mumbles, knowing full well that it is unlikely to be one, from my point of view and as a spectacle.

— Good match.

He serves and I under hit, the ball scarcely rising above the bottom of the net. He serves again and I over hit, the ball shooting beyond the table. This is voodoo ping-pong. Natural laws of physics inverted. I'm seeing black and yellow warning tape. Eventually I return a serve but his follow-up shot proves unplayable, the ball dying on me before I can play a shot.

I am not enjoying much more success with my own serve. I am serving too short. To serve long, flat and fast against long pippers is Simon's rule. Finally I obey it and Michel pops up his return, allowing me to execute a decent forehand smash. I repeat the serve and it works again. Some points at last, but I am playing catch up. Michel wins the set 6–11.

I begin the next set by foul serving. Inexcusable at this level. When Michel next serves I miss the ball altogether. He has reduced my confidence to that of a beginner. He scarcely needs to play at all! I try geeing myself up. This fails. 4–11. Damn. Damn.

Michel from Montpellier allows himself the briefest of smiles. But it is as if he has offended the Gods of Ping who, at the start of the third set, gift me two consecutive points: one ball flying off the table edge, another trickling over the net. Michel's not returning those. Unaccountably he misses two relatively easy smashes. Frustration gathers within him. I feed off it. I move better. I win the set 11–8. For the fourth I command myself not to serve short or enter into long rallies. If I allow one to develop he will as likely win it. I obey the command but Michel takes a 1–5 lead. I feel myself surrendering to gloomy prognostication. In the next rally he pulls out of making a shot. A ball from a nearby match must have strayed into our playing zone. I am wrong. Michel is limping towards me, hand extended. An explanation comes in a single word.

— Hamstring.

Inwardly thanking my lucky stars, I commiserate with him like the huge hypocrite I am. The Vis must be doing the same, having just witnessed Michel's long-pips expertise.

Michel is out of the tournament, but he respects the umpiring schedule, meaning he will umpire the next game, between the Vis.

Before returning to base camp I watch my future adversaries play their opening set. Fred Perry soon getting the upper hand, Marseille man lacking in consistency. He plays a succession of wild shots. It is a slovenly, rash way of playing that will surely cost him the match.

*

9.05 a.m.

I down half a pint of water and then chew contently on a fig. Despite Michel's forced abandonment, I am officially credited with a win. A win over a 1300 rated player! At one fell swoop I jump from 920 to 950. There are bands of points, these being gradations of ability. My goal next season is to extricate myself from the 850 to 1000 points band.

I can see that David is umpiring while Alain, having umpired the first game of his pool, is in action. He is up against a towel merchant. I don't mean a retailer in bathroom accessories. I mean one of those players who repeatedly reach for their towels ostensibly to remove facial sweat, but whose true intention is to disrupt an opponent's rhythm. Having recently lost to a towel merchant par excellence, Alain was probably wary of encountering another. Usually they hold no fear for Alain. But the last one, a slim and unnervingly silent player, timed his towel breaks to perfection, managing to irritate Alain without incurring a penalty from the umpire. This towel merchant, though, cannot cope with Alain's sidespin service. His returns are too high and Alain is whacking winners all over the table. His confidence is already shot. His play disintegrates. He can take all the towel breaks he likes, Alain isn't allowing his concentration to slip.

Point of fact: Towel breaks do not actually waste time. No playing time as such is lost. They prolong the period of non-playing time.

In tournaments between matches you have a lot of free

time: time to get fluids into you; time to physically recover from testing physical encounters, to attend to that slight cramp in your left calf; time to marvel at the absurdity of the situation you find yourself in.

How does a 53-year-old man come to be thinking about towel breaks during a game of table tennis on an exceptionally hot Sunday morning in May in the south of France?

Who or what is to blame?

Two years ago I was sitting at a café, reading *L'Équipe*. An article on table tennis got me thinking about a sport I had not played seriously in decades. Almost four of them!

It was thanks to friendly neighbours that I began playing at the relatively young age of ten. The Simmonds's had a table-tennis table in their garage. It was here that Joey Simmonds, a 14-year-old Led Zep aficionado, taught me how to play the basic shots, including how to smash the ball beyond an opponent's reach. It was instant gratification. The game was quick, as was the satisfaction it generated.

Around this time a friend at junior school, Simon Snell, announced that he was looking for a doubles partner. I eagerly responded, which is how I came to start playing on a more regular basis.

Simon's dad would take us along to the local Conservative Club whose basement had a well-stocked bar and some – most fiercely lit – snooker tables. Around which quiet men, armed with cues, treaded lightly as though stalking prey. Their fags smouldering in ash trays.

The basement also contained a table-tennis table, a most wonderful specimen supported on four mighty looking oak legs and the sole reason for us coming to the club. At the time I gave no thought to people's political affiliations. Simon and I were too young to have any ourselves.

Simon and I would practise together before teaming up to take on his dad. After the session Simon's dad would buy us each a glass of Coca-Cola. These training sessions and perhaps the pleasing novelty of Coca-Cola, resulted in Simon and me becoming the U12's County Doubles Champions. Shortly afterwards I was invited to join the club where Joey Simmonds played. The head coach, Gus Stevens, took a keen interest in me. Within months I was playing competitively.

It's a simple game, Gus had explained, provided you get the basics right. For which he had devised an elementary form of ping-pong notation. The game's grammar abbreviated.

Fd stands for forehand drive.
Bd stands for backhand drive.
Fp stands for forehand push.
Bp stands for backhand push.

— Like a four-stroke engine. Get these fundas licked and the engine will always bloody tick over.

What is it about coaches and their proclivity for using car engines for metaphors?

Fd Bd Fp Bp
Bd Fp Bp Fd
Fp Bp Fd Bd
Bp Fd Bd Fp
Fd Bd Fp Bp

This Gus made me repeat ad nauseum. On two occasions I really was sick.

Once Gus was satisfied I had mastered the four fundamentals, Gus taught me more advanced shots, which required a slightly more sophisticated system of notation.

Sbh stands for sliced backhand.
Fts stands for forehand topspin.
Flts stands for forehand looping topspin.

I practised and practised with the aim of achieving robotic constancy. It was flattering to be told I was a *natural* with great potential. A potential, alas, I never came to fulfil. This applied to other sports too. Gordon Hill, Man United's fleet-footed winger of the 1970s, said I was one of the best 9-year-old footballers he'd seen playing outside Manchester, which is a most unfortunate age to peak at a sport, for it was all downhill from there.

On Tuesday evenings Gus would take me, along with other boys, to play against clubs throughout the borough. Their teams mostly comprised players as old as Gus. Old codgers is how my 14-year-old self thought of such men. They had peculiar bats and even more peculiar styles of play. They had dodgy knees and seemed to move in slow motion. Yet against such players we suffered inexplicable defeats. Now, having become an old codger myself, I understand only too well what must have happened. For I employ all the guile I can muster to inflict defeats on teenagers in the leagues of the *Gard département*. You get the picture: wily old campaigner beats temperamental youth. Profiting also from their impetuosity.

Gus Stevens and Joey Simmonds were good coaches, in their different ways. Much later in life Joey became a successful tennis coach. Even before his family moved away, he was playing less table tennis in order to devote himself to tennis, a sport with considerably more earning potential. I will never forget him bringing into the garage a turntable upon which he repeatedly played *Whole Lotta Love*. Enjoyably recognisable as the *Top of the Pops'* theme tune.

Gradually the lure of table tennis lessened for me too. And, preoccupied by football, heavy metal and parties, I stopped playing competitively in my mid-teens. I continued to play 'for fun' since the Simmond's, in moving home, generously left us their worm-riddled table. These insect-bored perforations constituted a minor aesthetic blemish. Missing bits of table veneer, while causing the ball to bounce unexpectedly, probably helped develop my reflexes.

After reading that article in *L'Équipe* I made some enquiries and was told about a local club whose members met on Wednesday and Friday evenings in what was a former factory. There was space for eight tables, an unimaginable luxury in cities like Montpellier.

It was a late return. And taking up the sport again was strange. Not quite like riding a bike. Fortunately I'd retained enough muscle memory to play correctly. Never mind that my shots seldom went exactly where I intended.

It came as a surprise to learn that eleven points won

you the set instead of twenty-one, and that players took turns to serve every two points instead of five. The balls were slightly larger too, being perhaps of some benefit to someone whose eyesight has worsened slightly with age. Organisers, wishing to make table tennis more telegenic, marginally increased the size of the balls. For all that, the appeal of televised table tennis seems limited to hard-core fans of the sport. There has never been much money or prestige in table tennis.

Radio commentary is out of the question. The action is simply too fast. A commentator – in order to convey it – would require Gus Stevens-like abbreviations. The sport best appreciated by being present at the match itself; to stare in wonder at sheer speed and accuracy of top-class players. They say clarity of air collapses distance. Well, speed and crispness of shot has a similar effect.

At some moment during that first session I tapped into a residual memory of juvenile glory, and succeeded in smashing the ball off the table. Dopamine flowed and I was hooked again. Simon immediately saw that another player would be joining the club, someone with a healthy dose of competitive zeal.

At fifty-three you are generally more reflective as a person. Pompous and pretentious too. You end up trying to write about table tennis and making grandiose metaphysical claims. Supreme sport played at the mind/body interface. Ontologically, there seems to be a mind/body split. In the world of sport, Descartes rules ok; his dualism theory holding sway.

*

9.25 a.m.

Alain wins quickly. This was not unforeseeable.

He and I now watch David who is concentrating as hard as his mind/body will allow. Boy, does he need to. He is up against Galtier whose right knee is heavily strapped. There is a lot of weight/pressure to support. Despite his being immense (in both in height and girth) Galtier is a nimble mover. Each shot played with calm authority. The full balls, he drives. The short balls, he chops. He has a Zen-like discipline in selecting the right shot. When he plays, he plays. He gorges on a glut of David's high bouncing returns.

David's game is classically correct, but he is being dismantled by a player who is simply superior. Galtier blocks fractionally faster and makes few errors. David must attempt something out of the ordinary. But this is not in his nature. He obstinately adheres to his game plan. I feel for David, but it is hard not to be impressed by Galtier's tyranny at the table. David plays a low trajectory, hyper-sliced backhand that Galtier nonchalantly smashes away for a winner. He has no right to make such a shot. Yet make it he does.

Our defeated colleague joins us. Alain tries to humour him.

— There is a Chinese saying that 'defeat should be celebrated because in the process your opponent is educating you'.

— *Merde*, Alain. *Merde*.

*

9.35 a.m.

My next opponent is Pierre something or other, the more muscular of the Vis who likes to attack. I have just seen Marseille man play. The rallies will be short and sweet.

I am nervous. Simon would approve. If you aren't nervous, you do not care enough about winning, or to win.

Performance anxiety is normal enough. Pre-match nerves are to be expected and, to a certain extent, welcomed. Being very nervous while playing, however, is seldom a good thing. Any residue of nervous tension can be extremely debilitating to a ping-pong player. A player's overall performance is significantly impaired by just the slightest tightening of an arm muscle, with their every shot, thereafter, going a bit askew. Confidence fades along with their chance of victory.

Marseille man lost to Fred Perry, so, given Michel's abandonment, there is a lot riding on this match. Winning it would guarantee me a place in the knockout stages.

The protocol in warming up is not to smash outright winners, but Simon advises us to win these rallies all the same and gain a psychological edge. I concentrate hard during the forehand drive and backhand drive exchanges, doing my best not to be the one who strays.

Impose or be imposed upon. That is the law of this sport. Bloody Darwinian.

You must break the pattern of the others' dominance.

Once I was caught out by a player who could not land a single decent shot in the warm-up, but as soon as the match began he found his range. He could play all right. Pretty damn devious, he was, and five points to the good before I understood I had been hoodwinked. Now, winning pre-match rallies, I remind myself of that particular encounter.

Marseille man and I seem evenly matched. His forehand drives have more potency (spin) but my backhand is considerably more reliable.

You have a good backside, Simon once remarked, wanting to show off his English.

— Pardon.

— I like your backside.

I had to laugh. This was *Carry On* material. Such are the perils of literal translation.

— You mean backhand, Simon. Backside is your derrière.

Said with glee, pointing at my bum and his.

The start to the match is evenly contested. Neither he nor I can attain a significant lead. I am conscious I mustn't overdo serves to his backhand. He is getting better at returning them. At 9–9 it is anybody's set, but I have the advantage of serving. My first provokes a slight mis-hit, the ball ballooning up. I have all the time in the world to smash it beyond Marseille man's reach and earn myself a set point. Overly hesitant, I strike the ball marginally late. It misses the table by less than inch. 9–10. Shit Shit Shit. Such a mistake proves impossible to banish from my consciousness. What I do forget is counting to three before my next serve. My composure has gone. I serve hurriedly, and it is stillborn. The ball takes a deflection off the net and misses the table altogether. I hang my head in shame. Just as well that Simon isn't here to witness such ineptness.

As if stepping into Simon's shoes, Alain appears. He surprises me. Apart from my suicidal finish I am playing reasonably well, he reckons.

His counsel is succinct and clear.

— *Revers, revers, revers.*

Pulverise Marseille man's backhand. I do and it pays dividends. I win the set 11–7 and the next 11–6, much aided by Marseille man's increasing rashness. He throws the game in much the same manner he had against Fred Perry.

I am elated. The match lasted longer than that against Michel, but I feel not even a hint of tiredness. I've specially trained for today. Early morning jogs. Mountain walks. I am much fitter than I've been in years. Legs, says Simon, are your silent motor. They get scarce attention but they are doing all the heavy lifting. Literally, in Galtier's case.

Le Revers

Shortly after joining the club I was asked if I wanted to play for their second-string team. You bet, sign me up.

I was told to see a doctor since in France a health certificate is required to play in any official sporting league. I knew the club doyen, 87-year-old Jacky, had got one from his GP. It will be a breeze, I thought. But the young doctor I saw had other ideas. He put me through my paces. Squat thrusts and star jumps. Taking my pulse before and after.

— This isn't for the Foreign Legion, I said.

Without so much as a hint of a smile, he wrote out a certificate, authorising me to '*jouer ping-pong en competition*'. Then he charged me 22 euros for his time and professional sadism.

I had been expecting him to write *tennis de table*.

Later I learned that the French are rather partial to ping-pong.

Ping.

Apparently the sport's correct title in most of the world is table tennis. Yet prescribed correctness ought to be challengeable. To some people's ears table tennis sounds like a minor version of tennis, a belittling description.

You say table tennis and possibly think: hardly a sport for grown-ups is it.

Pong.

Does ping-pong, originally an Edwardian parlour game, really truly convincingly portray the sport as being one for grown-ups?

Ping-pong is, after all, the trademark of a children's toys manufacturer.

Ping.

At least ping-pong is not being compared (unfavoura-bly) to another sport. And the onomatopoeia connotes something of the sport's rhythmic essence.

An onomatopoeia for pedants:

ping (bat) ting (table) pong (bat) tong (table)

Imagine.

Fancy a quick game of ping ting pong tong.

*

I made my debut in a home match, played on the club's best (cornilleau) tables, reserved for such occasions. Alain had earlier removed their dust sheets with David getting out the scoreboards. My contribution had been to make the coffee. So as to ensure a warm welcome for our visitors whose all-round youthfulness took everybody by surprise.

My first opponent, an emaciated adolescent with greasy hair and chronic acne, exhibited no nerves whatsoever. Or emotions for that matter.

In contrast my body fizzed with nervous energy, even during the warm-up.

I avoided making sloppy shots, as did the youngster. Consequently, the exchanges were prolonged and his teammate, who was umpiring, had to signal, by way of coughing, that the match ought to get underway.

Having hidden the ball in one hand, the umpire put both hands under the table, asking me to guess which hand held the ball. I guessed wrongly but my opponent said I could serve first.

— *Merci.*

The gesture, Simon later explained, was not necessarily as chivalrous as it appeared. Players may have ulterior motives in allowing opponents to serve first. They might be wishing to convey their sense of superiority. Along the lines of no way mate are you on my level. They also ease the pressure on themselves since players are expected to win the points of their service.

As I am preparing to serve, Simon calls me over to the plastic barrier that delineates the playing zone.

— Don't rush anything, Bill. Take the time that needs to be taken. Nothing too fancy. Play as you have been doing against me. Win or lose, enjoy yourself.

Win or lose, enjoy yourself! Such words did not belong in Simon's lexicon. They were totally at odds with Simon's character. In training he harangued. (It turned out that he had mis-read a coaching manual, one dealing with counter-intuitive tactics.)

The adolescent was athletic. He hit stunning winners. But he played with a somewhat reckless verve. My sliced backhand generally got the better of his forehand looping topspin, his fetish shot. I defended adequately and won the set 11–8. It might be more accurate to say the youngster lost it. His teammates proceeded to give their charge a good talking to.

I had not expected there to be a break between sets. I stood awkwardly at the table. Simon sidled up to hand me a bottle of water. My gratitude was twofold. Drinking gave me something to do as well as quenching my thirst.

Simon complimented me on my composure.

— Great stuff, Bill. Keep heavy slicing the backhand and you have this in the bag. Don't change a thing.

It had not been my intention to do so.

It was my opponent who did all the changing, by transforming himself into a vastly superior version of his first-set self. He muffed fewer shots and executed more stunning winners. Shots with a very high tariff of difficulty.

And my response?

I buckled. My energy evaporated. My forehand push went on me. I could not even return his serves, undone by disguised – I assume in hindsight – side and top spin. A series of poor shots sapped my confidence. My legs tar slow. After he took the second set, the match turned into rout. Three sets (6–11, 3–11, 2–11) lost in approximately eight minutes. He was as emotionless in victory as he was in playing. Whether this emotional dumbness was an act I could not say.

Simon tried to console me. I had been beaten by a 'really decent player'. Alain was more critical.

— You mustn't let them gain confidence.

Them being the young players to whom Alain made it a personal rule never to lose.

A fortnight later I was freshly humiliated, beaten by a boy bundle of energy and earnestness a quarter of my age.

Simon had instructed me to serve short to make the youngster stretch.

— Outmanoeuvre the upstart. No mercy, Bill.

He had been reading a different manual.

I had not intended to show the boy mercy. But it was boy prodigy who outmanoeuvred me, expertly placing the ball beyond my reach.

Seldom will a player's size or physicality determine the game's outcome, a fact which makes for intriguing intergenerational duels.

It is the player's skill – with the bat – that counts the most.

What other sport can have a 12-year-old boy run rings round a fit quinquagenarian?

After each winning shot the boy punched the air with his fist and yelled out CHO! Meaning good point in Chinese.

Alain was not impressed.

— His coach should tell him to knock that on the head. Constant cho'ing will earn him few friends.

Apparently the boy was breaking table tennis etiquette. Only after winning an exceptionally hard-fought point should Cho be used. That is, sparingly. There were worse transgressions, though. Alain cited examples of players cho'ing at the top of their lungs after winning a point by an edge ball, net ball, or opponent's unforced error. Quite staggering breaches of decorum.

— When players do that to me I'm liable to lamp them.

I do not think Alain was speaking figuratively.

Regardless of the inappropriate cho'ing the boy is probably now playing at a very high level. Simon, though, was more circumspect in his judgement.

— He's good, but overcoached.

Pretty strange comment for a coach to make.

Let's pass on the actual set scores. Suffice to say I suffered a heavy defeat.

Fair to say that my first games in D1 of the Gard League did not go exactly to plan. I sulked discreetly.

Then I played a man my age sporting John Lennon glasses. Alain remembered playing him two seasons ago.

— Lennon specs. *Edgy* player, said Alain.

Like me then, I thought. But Alain had not meant the player was of a nervous disposition. He meant rather that Lennon specs aims to land the ball near the table edge.

— Misses a lot, added Alain.

An adversary who misses the table is a good adversary in my book. Indeed, he did not have the regularity to trouble my game. From the start I felt in control. I even had the presence of mind to recall (and obey) Simon's serving instruction: three breaths – one, two, three – to recollect your thoughts and serve. I was composed. My opponent was not. He was sweating profusely and, between points, having to wipe his glasses free of perspiration. They were slipping and constantly pushed back to the bridge of his nose. My glasses have never been a problem. I forget I am wearing them.

I played faster, Alain style, and accumulated more points. Confidence, a fickle friend, returned. All my shots were coming off. My inner chimp pumped fists in triumph. Time was on my side. Seeming to extend and allow me to hit balls hard and to precisely where I wanted.

Conversely, time seems to have accelerated for Lennon specs, forcing him to rush shots.

11–8, 11–6, 11–5. An emphatic victory in anyone's book. Endorphins flowed and a sense of well-being coursed through me.

Afterwards we had a match debrief. Alain, who had yet another zero in the loss ledger, said I acquitted myself reasonably well. Simon nodded but mentioned that while defending well with chops and reflex blocks, my performances were one dimensional. He concluded that I must attack more. I had squandered points that were mine for the taking. Instead of killing the rally, my cautious approach enabled opponents to re-seize the initiative. Could this explain why during my matches I experienced violent swings of mood? Simon reassured me that it was normal to feel like a natural born loser one minute and unbeatable the next.

— You're neither in reality. You have to train yourself not to get either too carried away with excitement or too down in the dumps.

Achieving such equanimity during actual play is not easy. Many players let rip to fully reveal their feelings. You need to be something of a trained stoic to treat – as Kipling famously recommended – Triumph and Disaster just the same.

After games it is equally hard neither to exult (over winning) nor despair (over losing.) Victory highs may last days, feelings of intense satisfaction to be fully savoured. My best matches stored in the memory for future musings; shots that can never unhappen.

Conversely morale-sinking defeats ruin weekends, the mental torture of replaying over and over squandered set or match points.

I improved fast under the guidance of Simon, a coach who lacks nothing in self-belief. He saw it as his mission to transfer some to me, along with an enviable set of table-tennis skills.

Six months ago I was making too many unforced errors, which Simon attributed to a lack of mental resolve. He thought I could acquire some if only I tried. Thinking that seemed deeply flawed to me.

— You're saying I lack will power because I lack the will power to find it?

He ignored my objection and, for the umpteenth time, commands me to repeat the following words: think positive, play positive. I recited the words in good faith but invariably found myself thinking: what if I am simply less talented than Simon gives me credit for?

This hardly counted as a positive thought.

Simon must be doing something right. This season I have 17 wins in 21 matches. A proof of my improvement.

*

10.15 a.m.

Defeating the dapper Fred Perry would mean topping the group. There would be some satisfaction in that, but more importantly it would mean avoiding Miguel, in the next (knockout) round, whose arms are indeed remarkably hairy.

There are players here more generous in their praise than Alain.

Miguel, I have gleaned, has the best backhand in the tournament.

He has eliminated the man stuck in the Twingo.

I begin with serves of moderate backspin which Fred Perry, in his overexuberance, topspins straight into the net. I return his first serve, fluking an edge. So when he foul serves I find myself 4 points up, just over one third of the way to winning the set. I retain a four-point advantage all the way to 9–5. An unassailable lead, I believe. Until I blow it.

Unaccountably I go into my shell, playing percentage

risk-minimising table tennis. The safer I play, the easier it becomes for Fred Perry. The lead narrows. At 9–8 I sense panic welling within me. Fred Perry is now playing with fluency, having probably thought at 9–5 down that he had nothing to lose. Struggling even to lay bat upon ball, I end up losing the set 9–11.

Six points lost in a row.

My opponent, having fully adapted to my playing style (whatever that is) believes that victory is now his for the taking. He is right too. A crash in confidence sees me lose the second and third sets 0–11, 1–11. Complete meltdown. I burn with humiliation. People must be thinking: who is the charity case and how the hell did he get to play in a regional?

Shed the negative emotions, Bill. That is what Simon would counsel. Easy to say. So hard to do.

— Look, Simon once explained, either it is within your ability to win the match or it is not. No point in getting upset or angry when the outcome is beyond your control.

He is naturally stoical that way. Simon the stoic.

I sit down alongside David and Alain who say nothing. Empty words of consolation will only make me feel worse. Fred Perry has made my body and brain ache. It is hard to accept such a heavy loss. Yet I cannot express too much disappointment. Not in front of David who will not be progressing into the knockout phase. I have qualified by default, thanks to Michel of Montpellier pulling a muscle. David has been unlucky, finding himself in a pool of players with Galtier and a Chinese chopster using small pips. Not that David ever seems unduly upset. And if he were, he would ask for the keys to Alain's car and go and sleep off his defeat. David has a calm persona. Maybe it is all the sleeping he does. He lives in a commune with a younger woman and their two small children. They live off the land when David is not working intermittently as an IT consultant. He gives me the impression of never having entered the mainstream of life. And of never intending to. He, Alain and I are all self-employed. Alain mends fridges. I sell second-hand books in English (with a Don Quixote-like stubbornness given that I am living in France). Table tennis seems an individualistic sport. The singles, that is. We all work for ourselves too. Perhaps there is something in that.

Alain wins his remaining matches with embarrassing ease. Shyler cannot live with the pace of play Alain imposes. He is floundering in an unfamiliar time zone. This is Alain's show. The Fast show. He operates in a different time zone, and his opponents' senses and reflexes must adjust, and quickly, if they are to deny him a speedy victory. For good measure Alain brings out his reverse spinning serves. Devious and coming at you like a cobra's lunge. He even plays a set of exhibition table tennis, unleashing looped forehands and executing smashed forehands that rent the very air. It feels good to be associated with someone so talented, so immersed in victories. What makes him able to play so fast?

A bionic arm?

Freakishly rapid muscle fibre twitching?

A superior flicker-fusion rate, enabling him to see more frames per second than players like me?

Do my shots appear to him as slow as a slide show!

The table is a mathematical space (nine feet by five). Call this a.

There is also its psychophysiological space. How it is perceived. Call this b.

Alain is patently mapping b. onto a. faster and more accurately than me.

*

11.00 a.m.

It is a straight knockout, now.

Should I change bat? Get out the new one?

Armed with a shifter sponge bat and wishful thinking. That is me.

Realistically I have zero chance of beating Miguel. Yet nothing is foretold, fluctuating fortune the stuff of life. Table tennis has no special immunity to bizarre improbabilities playing out. Like me defeating Miguel.

As Simon says. All cars can break down. (Motoring metaphor madness).

As David, the quasi hippy, says. The future is open until it happens. Man.

*

Last summer I trained hard. Bare chest trophied with sweat, still Simon did not lessen the tempo. I paused only to drink water straight from the tap.

— Less arm, more trunk.

I understand that Simon wants me swivelling into forehands, but it is difficult to iron out faults I probably acquired as a teenager. I am on a grail quest; to play a perfect series of shots. Breaking the habit of playing lazy shots is a challenge. I must rise to meeting it. Good technique pays dividends, and all the more so in the superior leagues.

Pure natural ability is a myth. So Matthew Syed and

Malcom Gladwell have convincingly written. Put in the hours and you will likely improve. So too your ability!

Since April the nights have been unseasonably warm. Simon had to open the windows, to induce cooling draughts. In daytime he shut the windows and drew the blinds, so as to repel both light and heat. Some stretching, then we played and played. There was (and remains) so much to learn. If only there were some top-level ping-pong software available and the technology to download it direct into my skull like Neo in *The Matrix*.

One evening Simon did something strange, sitting me in front of a mirror with the instructions to stare intently into my own eyes. Then he held a playing card just outside the boundary of my peripheral vision.

— Stare straight ahead and tell me Bill, what the card is.

He was wriggling it, but I could not tell if the card was red or black. It was only when the card was almost in front of me that I could identify it as the Ace of Spades.

— Body position, Bill. Body position. Get your head behind the ball and you'll see it better! Avoid any blind spots!

I try to recall the desultory instructions issued in training: hit the ball in the rising phase; bat angle needs to be almost vertical to table, to give topspin to counteract backspin; use body, not just arm to slam hit; chop harder, generate more backspin; smash harder, to smash off the effects of long pimples (long pips). Don't give the pip masters opportunities to play. Smash 'em off the bloody table; and Simon's favourite – stay at the table, no retreating.

My mind is sluggish. Come on I urge it. Con-centrate. Otherwise I will lose, in double quick fashion. Alain and Galtier are the kind of players who never allow this to happen. Even when they are out of form, they find ways of winning points; of staying in contention. The same cannot be said of me. Intermittently I suffer *passages à vides*. Meaning I haemorrhage points. Yet there is a part of me that still believes I can win today, with the important provisos of playing to the best of my ability and (as equally important) having a sufficient amount of luck with net calls and table edges. I am not alone. Probably the majority of entrants fall into the 'thinks he could win with certain provisos' category. There is a delusional aspect to this, of course, depending on the player's age, talent and training.

You are in a car and the rain is hammering down. You hesitate to get out. But when you do you find it is less bad than you had thought. And you don't really understand why. This is a little like the difference between observing and playing certain players. Some flatter to deceive. Like Miguel's fancy looking serves. They are easier to return than they look. Unfortunately the car/rain analogy does not apply to other aspects of his game.

My main strength – a reliably strong backhand – Miguel blunts by having a better one. Miguel needs a few rallies to get his eye in. Then he finds his cadence and it is curtains for me. For the first time in months I am truly outclassed. His shots, executed by that hairy right arm of his, are too fast for me to touch, let alone control. I cannot even pretend to put up meaningful resistance. I must force myself not to succumb to the temptation of playing rash hit and hope stuff. But what have I got to lose. Yet I am unable to play even with the freedom of the condemned.

It is a horrible sensation of helplessness. Knowing defeat is inevitable. No matter how much physical and mental effort you are prepared to put in. I am made to feel like a clumsy bag of bones. I will pass on the set scores.

Shit, it is sinking in. Defeat, that sour negation of victory. I am out. OUT. I hate the feeling. I feel like giving up. But I will not. The pain of defeat, I know, eventually vanishes (as does the joy of victory). And I will continue getting up at six on Sunday mornings, to be driven seventy-odd miles to meet up with blokes (in the main) to bash balls about on a table. And when a new season starts, I will turn up to training with fresh hope. Never mind that my body will be older, my reflexes slightly slower, or that some of my contemporaries have pulled muscles simply eating toast for breakfast. The health capital we had as youngsters has gone. Gerard broke an ankle tying his trainers' laces. Three months back I over-did the follow through on a forehand drive. I missed the ball, striking a direct hit to the eyebrow. Blood spurted everywhere; onto face, hands and the table.

Outwardly I acknowledge such facts, but inwardly I am putting up resistance. Between June and September, I feel keenly the emptiness of post and pre-season Sundays; their lack of spice. I am so not ready to renounce the world of competitive sport. Look at Jacky, 13 years shy of a hundred and still training regularly when he isn't re-designing ping-pong robots and complaining about dirty floors.

— *Regarde ça*, Bill. Preventing the balls from being fired out. I'm going to have to sort out the cleaners.

We congregate in halls and sports gyms, to play in local leagues and temporarily escape work and the inanity of day to day domesticity. It is a circuit of sorts; friendships re-established, animosities too. The talk is of previous team encounters, epic games of yesteryear and legendary comebacks. (Eight match points saved. Eight!). New bats flourished, catalogues shared and pored over; the relative merits of varying rubbers and pimpleness argued over with a theological nicety.

— Play with that and we won't have any decent rallies.

— It's the only bat I have.

— You give me the pip.

— Stop taking the pip.

There is the mandatory ribbing:

— You need to change your rubbers. It's sliding, the top sheet's gone. I'll show you some good wrist strengthening exercises!

When the banter stops the games begin.

When the games end, the banter begins.

A cycle of sorts. The atmosphere is cordial, especially during *le aperitif*, emotions valiantly concealed; defeats being keenly felt until we next have an opportunity to play. Typically the talk is of previous encounters, epic games of yesteryear and those legendary comebacks. Eight match points saved. Eight! At some point somebody will work out that the taciturn baldy is *un étranger*. And I will then explain that Wales is not the same country as Scotland, and certainly not a part of England. The temptation is to drink all that is offered, especially if I have played well, but I try not to. Alain, who is blessed with a giant bladder, is not inclined to stop for our peeing needs.

Le Smash

11.25 a.m.

Semi-final. Alain v Balkoney.

It is to be a classic collision of styles: chop meister versus ball blaster.

As a chop meister *par excellence* and occasional towel merchant, Balkoney has the potential to seriously trouble Alain. His tactic will be to wear Alain down.

They warm up until the umpire asks if they are ready. Both men nod. Alain, taut with antipathy and concentrated energy, is so up for this. Balkoney looks thoroughly psyched up, too. Both men certainly intend to give it their – quite literally – best shot.

Play.

There is a mantra Simon recites to us.

— Go for the lines. Safety's for losers. Don't cede the initiative. Go for the lines. Safety's for losers. Don't cede the initiative. Go for the lines. Safety's for losers. Don't cede the initiative.

Alain respects it to the letter. He comes out all guns blazing, his big forehands working like a dream.

As well as smoking inordinate quantities of tobacco, Balkoney distinguishes himself by showily tossing the ball high before serving. Alain disdainfully puts these serves away. Balkoney side-sliced returns are not earning him easy points either. Alain deals with them before seizing on the slightest opportunity arising to smash the ball as hard as he can. Alain has got what he wants, a stop start match, staccato rallies. Even this early into proceedings Balkoney is fighting to keep self-doubt at bay. He resorts to a towel break but makes a tactical mistake. Instead of sticking to his naturally 'defensive' game, he attempts to outgun Alain. His shots fly well wide of the table. Alain takes the first set 11–7.

Balkoney's confidence incrementally seeps away with Alain taking a 6–3 lead in the second set. Balkoney becomes verbally aggressive, but this is mostly self-directed.

Then he receives a little help from Jammy Bastard, the patron saint of fluked shots. Three consecutive net snags meaning three consecutive points. Riled by this flurry of misfortune, Alain overly attacks. He makes unforced errors and Balkoney appears suddenly galvanised. His defensive chops are more controlled. Alain's shots start missing their target. Perhaps a sign of fatigue. Ultra-attacking shots require high energy input.

Alain desires a slug fest, but Balkoney sensibly is refusing to be drawn into one. His chance of winning the point inversely proportional to the ferocity of Alain's strokes. This is not like Alain. Cold, precise, hard and fast is what his game is about. His play has become frenetic. The harder he hits, the more likely Balkoney wins the point. Having acrobatically retrieved a series of Alain's slam hits, Balkoney then nails a blinding backhand to take the set 8–11. He has levelled the match. He is successfully disrupting Alain's game, seeding doubt.

Alain must adapt; change his style, using guile and ball placement instead of raw power. Is he capable? He so seldom has need to.

At the start of the third set Alain's disguised sidespin serve has Balkoney dead batting into the net, and snarling in frustration. It sets the tenor of the rest of the set. Increasingly Alain wrong-foots his opponent. All of sudden it is Balkoney's game that is disintegrating. There is a fatal hesitation to his movements. Balkoney is stalling. His chopped returns, landing in the middle of the table, are comfortably despatched by Alain.

Alain executes a few shots of showy extravagance. He is beginning to enjoy himself, finding unanticipated angles; the ball taking scything parabolas. The flailing bat seems a natural extension of his hand. He is outrunning himself. His play flaunts Newtonian laws; Einsteinian shots that curve, warp and ripple, and unplayable. The third set is comfortably won.

Balkoney delays the start of the next set by cleaning his bat with pedantic thoroughness.

— Won't help, whispers Alain.

— Wanker.

— Wanker.

The gloves are off. Balkoney's blood is up, a dispute inevitable. The umpire says nothing. Is he deaf or simply too bored to intervene?

In the set itself he finally reprimands Balkoney for taking a prolonged towel break, which does not succeed in disrupting Alain's rhythm. In frustration at this and the score (9–4 in Alain's favour), Balkoney flings his bat into the air. It careens into a barrier. Ping-pong is adversarial, but this is bang out of order. The spectators are stupefied.

Balkoney storms out of the building. Undoubtedly to smoke a cigarette. Not a celebratory one, though. No nationals for him.

La Serviette

I missed the Shyler–Miguel quarter final. Shyler won. Amazingly Miguel had trouble with his backhand. Couldn't handle the anti-top on Shyler's.

Shyler's semi against Galtier was at the same time as Alain's. I caught glimpses of the exchanges. Amazingly Shyler took the first set. But Galtier, having adjusted to Shyler's ultra-defensive style, grew in confidence. Shyler did not have an alternative game to revert to. Confidence is mutable; Galtier's snowballed, Shyler's evaporated. Galtier had the measure of him. At the end Shyler would not even have been capable of hitting a football, such were the Jedi mind tricks Galtier employed.

*

11.45 a.m. Final. Fabre v. Galtier.

So the tournament favourites have made it to the final. Men who hate losing as much as they love winning. Which partly accounts for them making it this far. There is another, equally important reason, though, which is that they happen to be bloody good exponents of the game!

For the final there is what you could charitably call a crowd, mainly comprising tournament participants. There is no prize money. With both men assured of the prestige of winning a place in the nationals, this game is exclusively about honour and bragging rights.

The tournament referee, thoroughly offended by Balkoney's antics, has chosen to umpire the final. She does not look the sort to stand any nonsense.

Alain and Galtier warm up. There is no joking. Might the occasion be getting to them? Maybe they are simply tired. There is tension in the hall. The match is difficult to call. The start to it is error strewn. Both players unused to having such speed-gun opposition. Balls fly straight into the net. There is no time for looping drives. Alain starts serving long and hard. He goes into full ball bludgeoning mode. So does Galtier. This is *blitzkrieg* ping. Both men believing offence is the best form of defence. Shades of Xu Xin v Wang Hao 2012.

Galtier makes fewer mistakes. Between points he rubs his bandaged leg. After winning the first set 6–11 he sits down to rest his leg. It is in his interest to win in three straight sets. Which is feasible given that Alain's timing is awry. There is no snap to his play. He looks sluggish. His face has the drowsiness that effort and stress may induce. Energy, concentration and willpower are sporting goods that can be quickly drained. Even following the rallies is tiring to watch. I find myself eating my last fig. Alain turns down my offer of chocolate. Neither David nor I know what to say, and the second set is more of the same.

— *JE SUIS PAS LA*!

Alain's cry of frustration has certain philosophical implications. Not that he is in any favourable mood right now to reflect upon them. Galtier smirks. *Il est la*. That is for sure. And making the most of his huge reach. Alain seems to have lost his instinct for the game; knowing how to place balls where an opponent least appreciates them. Alain has superior fleetness of foot, and a lower centre of gravity. But he is not making it count. He brings out his reverse spinning serve, which Galtier pulverises.

Alain loses the second set by the same score as the first. Things are desperate.

Over here Alain. HERE.

The caller is me – his humble protégée. He would not think of himself as needing a coach. No matter. He needs a dose of Simon's medicine.

— Alain, for fuck's sake buck up. Disrupt his rhythm before he disrupts yours. What is it that Simon's always saying? Attack early but not rashly. At least make him move about. Short. Long. Short. Long. Come on, shake the sluggishness out of your legs.

Alex Ferguson would be proud of me. Alain crouches with a look of renewed determination, which, coupled with a what-the-heck approach, seems to unsettle Galtier. Alain outguns him in the early exchanges of the third set. This is the Alain I know, the destroyer of players' reputations. By imparting extra spin to his shots in general, Alain has Galtier in some difficulty. Galtier's blocking shots go astray, just missing the table. Ping-pong is a sport of such fine margins.

Galtier changes tactics, determined to attack first, so as to take his destiny into his hands. If he makes the shot, he will invariably win the point. Such an ultra-attacking stance is not without risk. For one thing, it is harder to land the ball on the table. Indeed, Galtier is losing him more points than he is winning. Alain wins the set. He is still very much in this game. Yes. Come on.

The fourth set begins with Alain and Galtier displaying freakishly high levels of skill, as though making space–time conform to their wishes. Everyone in the hall is now watching. It seems to resurrect in us all the hopes we once had as youths. Sport at this level, so spirit enhancing. A few friends of Galtier are here, cheering on their man. David and I do likewise for Alain. The majority of spectators, however, are non-partisan. Both players equally appreciated.

Galtier is playing less recklessly than the previous set, but, from 3–2 up, he finds himself 3–6 down, Alain having executed a series of stunning backhands. Galtier can't reach these balls, let alone attempt to block them back. Between points Galtier is rubbing his leg gingerly. Perhaps preparing the excuses. His countenance is not exactly gloomy, but it is certainly less bright than it was. I become over-excited when Galtier, trailing 5–9, throws the set by attempting two ludicrously ambitious smashes. David, though, has misgivings, muttering something about Galtier conserving energy for the fifth and final set. And then I leave. This is pure cowardice. I go to the toilets and find an empty cubicle, and remain there until there is the sound of heavy and sustained applause. It is not long before someone wants to use the toilet for its proper purpose, and I must venture out to learn who has won.

*

Alain is driving us back and in the boot of his car, wedged between our bags, is a silver-plated cup. He is sated with Pernod and victory. I am chilled in the front seat. The *Gilets Jaunes* have dismantled all the speed cameras.

I put on a CD. *Speed King*. Deep Purple. Had to be.

'I'm a speed king you go to hear me sing,
 I'm a speed king see me fly.'

Alain the conqueror and I sing along. David, with ear-muffs, dozes in the back. Earlier, he'd filled me in on Alain's fifth-set stroll. 11–2. 11–2! Alain having made a deft tactical move, positioning himself slightly closer to the table, so as to mess with Galtier's timing. By the time Galtier figured out what was happening it was too late for him to rally. *Les carottes sont cuites pour lui*!

I will be making another late return. The family will have finished Sunday lunch. Hope they saved me some roast potatoes. I am running low on fuel. As Simon would say.

Misc. Notes.

Bat v racket. Bat, for me. In France it is racquets.

And paddles? Surely not. We're not members of some bloody boating club.

I am just showing my age.

Bats are red and black. One side covered with red rubber and the other black. In between, some laminated wood. Most players use red for forehand, black for backhand.

I wrongly assumed red rubber always to be the 'faster'. Simon set me right, explaining this isn't necessarily the case. Apparently the current trend among pros is to use black 'faster' rubber on their forehand.

Regulations specify that one side of a bat must be red while the other must be black. This allows a player to see what side of a bat hits the ball mid-play. These were brought in to prevent players from twiddling the bat to make it impossible to tell which side was hitting the ball.

Players still attempt such subterfuge with red and black bats, which Simon calls 'The Stendhal Switch'.

There are four types of blade handles: flared, straight, anatomical and conical. Simon recommended I limit my choice to one! A flared handle.

The Chinese have got this right. A flared handle allows you to hold the handle loosely.

Apparently by tightening your grip as you hit the ball lends a winning snappiness to your playing style.

Anatomical and conical were rejected out of hand. (Sorry, unintended pun). These handles don't allow you sufficient flexibility of the wrist or, as Simon says rather grandiosely, the freedom of the wrist. These handles adversely affect your transitional play, i.e. alternating forehand and backhand shots.

Shot or stroke?

Shot, for me. There's no time to gallivant about and play strokes. The ball struck in an instant.

The game of table tennis. The sport of table tennis. These sentences seem virtually interchangeable. Yet game implies recreation with the emphasis on enjoyment. Sport is something more serious, the emphasis on competition. Which is the only way Simon relates to table tennis.

He cannot understand that people play table tennis as a game. Recreation, the word, in Simon's mouth is unashamedly pejorative.

Was Whiff-Whaff ever in the running as an alternative name for the sport?

No.

PARTHIAN   Journeys

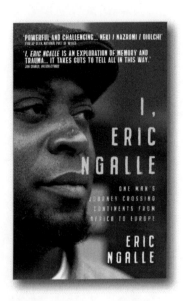

I, ERIC NGALLE:
One Man's Journey Crossing Continents from Africa to Europe
ERIC NGALLE

ISBN 978-1-912109-10-4
£9.99 • Paperback

'Powerful and challenging...
neki / nazromi / diolch!'
– Ifor ap Glyn,
National Poet of Wales

JUST SO YOU KNOW:
Essays of Experience
EDITED BY HANAN ISSA, DURRE SHAHWAR & ÖZGÜR UYANIK

ISBN 978-1-912681-82-2
£9.00 • Paperback

'Smart, bold and fresh – these are voices we need to hear'
– Darren Chetty, author, and contributor of *The Good Immigrant*

'This probing, honest and illuminating collection of essays is of course very timely but it's also one of the best books published in Wales in many a moon.'
– Jon Gower, Nation.Cymru

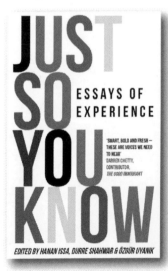

Also by William Rees . . .

THE LONELINESS OF THE LONG DISTANCE BOOK RUNNER

WILLIAM REES
ISBN 978-1-906998-92-9
£7.99 • Paperback

The Loneliness of the Long Distance Book Runner recounts the trials, joys and tribulations of selling second hand books: finding a valuable first edition gathering dust on a Parisian pub shelf, opening bookshops in Montpellier, Paris, Bangor, trading books with a holidaying Ian McEwan or Alan Sillitoe, and running for the door after finding yourself trespassing in a wealthy Moroccan's private library...

Full of quirky anecdotes and literary odds and ends, these unique insider's tales, inspired by Bill's time in the trade, are sure to spark the imagination of every book-lover who picks it up.

'Books are Rees' obsession, not just his living. Every search through an insect-infested crate of battered and mouldy hardbacks and paperbacks starts with a dream of finding the rarest of first editions by a celebrated author, preferably with a dust-jacket.'
– *Western Mail*